Here to Help

VET

James Nixon

Photography by Bobby Humphrey

W

FRANKLIN WATTS
LONDON • SYDNEY

Franklin Watts
First published in Great Britain in 2016 by The Watts Publishing Group

Credits
Series Editors: James Nixon and Paul Humphrey
Series Designer: D. R. ink
Photographer: Bobby Humphrey
Produced for Franklin Watts by Discovery Books Ltd.

Dewey number: 636.089
HB ISBN: 978 1 4451 4017 9
Library eBook ISBN: 978 1 4451 4019 3

Printed in China

Franklin Watts
An imprint of
Hachette Children's Group
Part of The Watts Publishing Group
Carmelite House
50 Victoria Embankment
London EC4Y 0DZ

An Hachette UK company
www.hachette.co.uk

www.franklinwatts.co.uk

Acknowledgements: BigStockPhoto: p.14 bottom (ZayacSK).

The publisher and packager would like to thank Holmer Veterinary Surgery, Hereford, for their help and participation in this book.

Contents

Words in **bold** are in the glossary on page 24.

I am a vet

Hello!

My name is Nafisa and I am a vet. My job is to help people keep their pets healthy. I treat lots of sick and injured animals every day.

?

What types of animals do vets help?

Many other staff work at our **surgery**. This is Nicole. She is one of our vet nurses. She helps me look after the animals.

Pearl is a receptionist. She welcomes pets and owners into the waiting room. Pearl answers the telephone and makes **appointments** for my patients.

Checking my patients

My first job each day is to check the **hospitalised** pets with Nicole. These patients are not well enough to go home and have stayed overnight at the surgery.

Rufus is looking much better today!

Why do you think vets need nurses to help them?

We make sure the animals are eating and drinking properly. We also check the **temperature** and **heartbeat** of some of the animals.

Bert had an **operation** yesterday. His leg was injured and had to be stitched up. I examine Bert's leg to make sure that the stitches are still in place.

Medicines and instruments

Rufus needs two tablets, twice a day.

To help some animals get better, I have to decide which medicines to give them. I tell Nicole which medicines should be **prescribed** to each patient.

Nicole counts out the correct amount of tablets in the medicine store.

I have lots of special instruments to do my job. Here are some of them.

Stethoscope – I use this to listen to an animal's heart and breathing.

Thermometer – I use this to check an animal's temperature.

Otoscope – I use this torch to look inside a patient's ears and mouth.

Nail clippers – I use these to stop a pet's claws getting too long.

Syringe – I use syringes to put some medicines into a patient.

Which of these instruments have you seen before?

My first appointment

My first appointment is with Flossy the rabbit and her owner, John. She sits in her pet carrier in the waiting room.

Flossy has runny eyes, which can be caused by teeth that have grown too long. First, I weigh her to check that she is eating well.

I use my otoscope to examine Flossy's teeth and to check that they haven't grown too long.

Flossy's teeth look fine, so I think she has an eye **infection**. I give her some **antibiotic** eye drops.

? How does a rabbit keep its teeth from growing too long?

Flossy also needs a **vaccination**. Vaccinations protect animals from diseases. I give Flossy the vaccination using a needle and syringe.

More appointments

My next appointment is with a dog called Molly. She has been sick and is not eating.

I feel Molly's stomach with my hands to check for a blockage.

She hasn't touched her food.

Molly has a sickness bug. The owner holds Molly still while I **inject** some medicine to make her feel better.

Spike also has tummy problems. He has eaten fruit cake. The cake contained raisins, which are **poisonous** to dogs.

I put Spike on a **drip**. The drip will slowly inject fluid into his body. This will protect his **vital organs** while he is unwell.

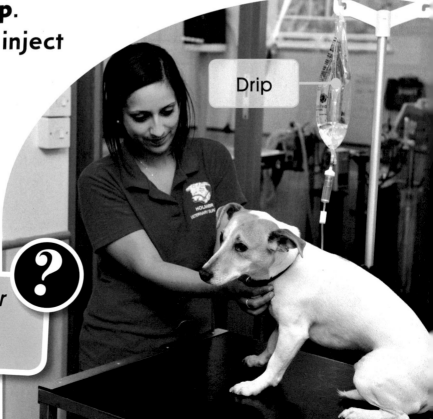

Drip

?

What foods can your pets eat and what should they not eat?

Scanning

Tony is another vet at the surgery. He is **scanning** a dog called Tammy to see if she is **pregnant**.

Tony scans Tammy using an instrument called a probe. This is called an **ultrasound**. It produces an image on a computer screen showing the inside of the animal.

I can see three puppies!

Probe

Elsa has been hit by a car. She has been badly injured.

First I send Elsa to sleep. Then I use an X-ray machine to take photographs of her bones. This will show me if any bones are broken.

I wear a special gown to protect me. It stops my body being **exposed** to the X-rays.

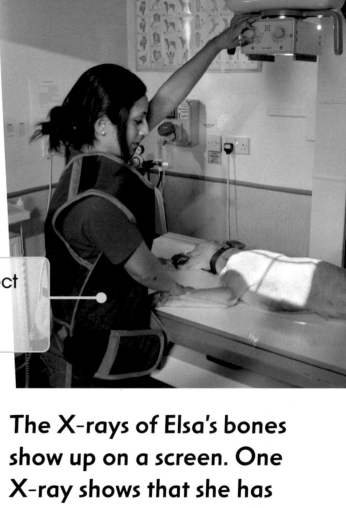

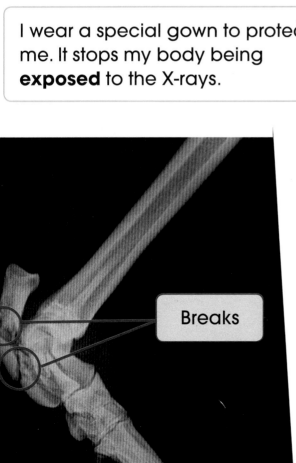

Breaks

The X-rays of Elsa's bones show up on a screen. One X-ray shows that she has broken her leg in two places.

?

Have you ever had an X-ray? If so, what did you have X-rayed?

Operations

Elsa needs an operation to fix her broken leg.

Before an operation it is important that I wash my hands well. Then I put on a pair of surgical gloves and a clean **scrub top**.

?

Why is it important for a vet to be clean before they operate?

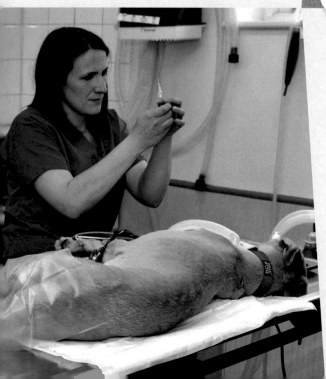

Angie, another vet nurse, is preparing some medicine. This will ease the pain when Elsa wakes up.

After I have operated on Elsa, Angie wraps a bandage around Elsa's leg. This will keep the leg supported while it heals.

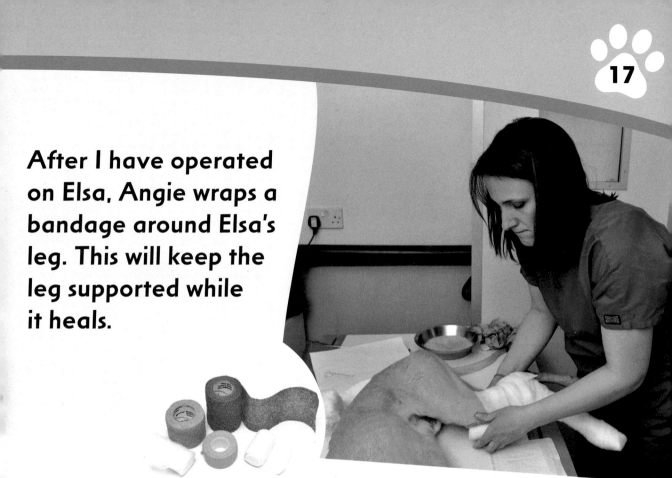

My next operation is on a cat. This operation is called a spay — it stops the cat from having any kittens.

Making phone calls

Every day I have lots of phone calls to make. Owners want to know that their pets are safe and well.

If I decide that a patient's treatment needs changing, I must let the owner know. Owners also ring me for advice.

The operation went well!

On some animals, I carry out blood tests, or take other **samples** to check for illness. The nurse puts the test results in a file. I look the results up and ring the owners to tell them the news.

Sometimes I use a **microscope** to check samples of skin for **parasites**, such as lice and mites; or blood for signs of infection.

Why do vets use a microscope to look at samples?

Out and about

Some pets can't be brought to the surgery. The owner may be too old to travel or the pet may be too sick. I visit these pets at their homes.

In the evenings and at weekends, when the surgery is shut, I often work 'on call'. This means I must keep my phone by me and be ready to rush out to any emergencies.

I also visit farms to treat animals such as cows, sheep and horses. Today, I am testing a **herd** of cows for a disease. I do these tests often so that the farmers can stop the disease from spreading.

Why do you think the cows are being moved through this metal cage?

Helping animals

I really enjoy being a vet. I work with a great team of people who help me do my job.

Most of all, I enjoy helping animals get better when they are sick and helping them stay healthy.

I really enjoy my job!

When you grow up...

If you would like to be a vet, here are some simple tips and advice.

What kind of person are you?

- You are friendly and enjoy speaking to people
- You are interested in science and how animals' bodies work
- You are prepared to work with sick and injured animals
- You are practical and like working with your hands
- Most of all, you enjoy looking after and helping animals.

How do you become a vet?

You will have to study science subjects at GCSE (Scottish Standard Grades) and at A Level (Scottish Highers). You will also have to study veterinary medicine at university for five years.

Answers

P4. Vets help all sorts of animals, both big and small. Some common animals that vets help are: cats, dogs, rabbits and hamsters. Some vets help unusual pets, such as parrots and lizards. Some vets help farm animals, such as cows, horses and sheep.

P7. Vet nurses perform a wide range of jobs to help the vets care for sick animals. These include feeding, giving medicines and helping the vets during operations.

P11. A rabbit's teeth never stop growing. Chewing on grass and hay wears the teeth down to the correct length.

P16. Vets wash their hands before surgery to stop the spread of infection to the patient.

P19. Microscopes are used to see things that are too small to be seen with the naked eye.

P21. The cage is used to hold the cows safely while they are treated.

Were your answers the same as the ones in this book? Don't worry if they were different, sometimes there is more than one right answer. Talk about your answer with other people. Can you explain why you think your answer is right?

Glossary

antibiotic a substance that can destroy and stop the growth of harmful bacteria

appointment an arrangement to meet at a set time

drip a bag of fluid, tube and needle that is used to slowly inject a patient with a liquid, drop by drop

exposed with no protection or shield

heartbeat the pulsing of the heart

herd a group of cattle or other animals that are kept together

hospitalised describes animals that are kept at the surgery to be cared for because they are too unwell to go home

infection disease caused by germs or bacteria

inject force a fluid into the body by piercing the skin

microscope an instrument that is used to make small objects look bigger

operation to use instruments to repair damage inside the body

organ a part of the body that performs a specific job, such as the eye, kidney or heart

parasite a living thing that lives and feeds on, or in, another animal

poisonous containing poison, which can harm or kill

pregnant carrying developing young in the body

prescribed instructed to use a medicine or other treatment

sample a small part of something taken to be tested

scanning taking images of the body with special medical equipment

scrub top a protective piece of clothing worn by vets during an operation

surgery the place where a vet works; also another name for an operation

syringe a tube with a nozzle that can suck up or squirt liquid, often fitted with a needle for injecting fluids into the body

temperature the level of heat inside the body

ultrasound sending waves of sound into an animal to produce an image of the inside of the body

vaccination a medicine that can help prevent a particular disease

vital necessary for life

Index